Incorporating:

Step by Step Guide to S Corps, C Corps, LLCs and LLPs

Written by Susan Kilmer

Introduction

I wanted to start off for thanking you for taking an interest in this book.

The main purpose of **_LLCs: Step by Step Guide to Incorporating_** is

to assist both the aspiring entrepreneur and seasoned business owner alike

better understand the difference between business entities such as sole

proprietorship, partnership and corporations.

The average individual knows through word of mouth and hearsay that they

should incorporate, but very few know what that actually means, when they

should incorporate, which entity they should choose and the obligations

that come alone with incorporating.

My goal for this start up guide is for you to have a basic understanding of

what incorporation is, the various business entities, the advantages and

disadvantages of each and for you to know enough to choose if and when

you should incorporate.

By the time you read the entire book, you will have a better understanding

of incorporating, which entity you will choose, the obligations of your choice and how to properly file with the appropriate government agency.

Enjoy!

Chapter 1

What is Incorporation?

Incorporating in simple terms is the act of splitting you and the business you own as separate entities – legally. This means that when a corporation your business assets can only be affected by the activities of business and does not affect your personal assets.

A corporation is considered a legal person in the eyes of the law. It can pursue actions and perform activities such as filing lawsuits, entering in contracts and agreements, buying and selling property or assets and can even be taxed. It has the almost the same rights as the business owner him or herself.

It's most prized value is that a corporation protects its owners from personal liability for business debts and obligations--within reason due to there being certain exceptions but we will go into that in later chapters.

The corporation is considered an artificially created legal entity that exists separate and apart from the business owners or those who created it and carry on its operations.

Before we get into the different entities a business can form, let's get into what you need to think about before you choose the proper legal form.

Factors to Consider

When deciding on the proper entity you want to set up your business to form into, you have to think about several factors as each of these factors influence which business entity you should pick. Factors include:

- **Your vision regarding the size of your business** – the bigger the business the more you will have to protect personally and business wise.

- **The nature of your business** – certain industries have certain operations that benefit more from certain business entities than others.

- **The level of control you desire** – Having entire control vs. sharing control determines whether you stay a Sole Proprietorship (non-corporation), Partnership (Sharing Ownership) or a Corporation (Formal Governing body w/ processes) that you will have to adhere to even if you are the only person working in the business.

- **Business vulnerability to lawsuits** – If your business is more susceptible to lawsuits such as the medical, child care and food based industries then it is important to form into a corporation to protect your personal assets from business assets.

- **Amount of non-business personal assets the ownership has** – Again if you have a lot of personal assets to protect such as real estate, assets, savings accounts, and 401Ks you will want to protect them by incorporating. If you aren't incorporated and are a Sole Proprietorship or Partnership, if your business runs into a lawsuit and your company loses, your personal assets will be affected.

- **Tax implications of different ownership structurers** – Different business entities have different tax obligations. Know your possible tax obligations and if it an obligation you can financially handle.

Chapter 2

Importance of Each Business Formation

According to some statistics, there is a surprising position relation of Proprietorships, Partnerships and Corporations in the United States. According to some graphs, Proprietorships are the most numerous representing 72% of all US organizations. Although, Proprietorships represent 66% of the most profitable companies, Corporations represent 82% of the companies that are earning the highest revenue amount.

Other realizations include:

- **Proprietorships** appear to be the most profitable business entity and received 10% of profits on only about 4% of revenues.

- **Partnerships** accounted for 6% of revenues and 24 percent of profits.

- **Corporations** received only 66% of the profits on about 82% of the sales

Why is any of this important?

Understanding the genetic makeup of each of the common business entities and the performance trends of the small business community will provide you the knowledge and data that you need to make the best legal decisions for your company.

It shouldn't be a hasty thing to rush into incorporation and due diligence must be performed in order to eliminate a lot of potential mistakes new business owners typically make that can be detrimental and costly to your new business.

Problems can be avoided with the proper knowledge, planning and systems in place for the business starts.

Chapter 3

Most Common Business Entity Options

There are a variety of business entities that exist and in this book we will only be covering the characteristics of the most common ones that are available to for profit companies. We will not be going into nonprofit entities or the new trend of Corporation, Sub Chapter B.

Business structures may different states but we will be talking about the most important entities, also known as business structures:

- **Sole Proprietorship** – Easiest and most common business structure as this is the default you are getting into if you are starting a business by yourself without any partners. This business entity is more common place as more individuals desire to go into business for themselves without having anyone to share the responsibilities **and** the profits.

- **General Partnership** – Is the most similar to Sole Proprietorship but the difference is that it contains multiple owners (min of 2).

- **Limited Partnership** – Similar to General Partnership but there is at least one (1) general partner and one (1) limited partner. Limited partner typically provides capital but their liability is limited. Suitable for those who want no operational responsibility but wants to reap in the financial rewards.

- **Corporations**

  - **Sub Chapter C** – Some similar to LLC and Sub Chapter C. Difference between this entity and other is the double taxation requirement. We will go into how despite the double taxation, there are some advantages to forming into this entity.

  - **Sub Chapter S** – Some similarities to LLC and Sub Chapter C. This is one of the corporation entities that enable you to separate your personal assets from business assets.

- **Limited Liability Corporation (LLC)** – Similar to a Corporation and contains unique characteristics as well. It has a lot of similar structure features as a corporation but is not obligated to perform a lot of the same duties.

In the following chapters, we will be going into each entity in more detail and will also talk about the advantages, disadvantages and brief explanations of some necessary obligations of each entity.

Chapter 4

Sole Proprietorship

A sole proprietorship is the most common business structure, the easiest business structure and yet the most costly. Not only is it costly financially but also because it's more susceptible to risk as there are no personal asset protections in place.

The main requirements to be a Sole Proprietorships besides being in one by default, a business must have the required operating permits and documents which include a business license for the city they are operating in, but also a Fictitious Business Name (FBN) aka *Doing Business As (DBA)*, any industry required permits/licenses, sellers permit and etc. If you would like more information regarding what each of these items are, please see my other book: **Starting a Small Business – Step by Step Guide to Business Ownership.**

To avoid using your social security number and having it associated with the business, you can file for an Employee Identification Number (EIN).

You do not have to have an employee or be in the middle of hiring one in order to file for an EIN.

This process is free and takes a few minutes. It is important to know which business entity you are currently in when filing for an EIN because it is one of the first questions on the form. Once you submit the form, you will be issued an EIN number which is a business identification number (similar to an individual's Social Security Number).

In this business structure, the owner has complete control as there is no other business, entity, board of directors, officers that the owner has to report to. The downside is, as the owner with no protection (other than business insurance – if it has enough coverage) that you are susceptible to losing any assets if you are involved in a lawsuit.

You do not need to fill out any separate tax returns for the business, all you will do is to file your regular 1040 tax form and including a Schedule C.

Chapter 5

General Partnership

A general partnership is similar to a Sole Proprietorship including its characteristics such as above, except it is a legal structure that includes 2 people. Think of it as a 2 man sole proprietorship:

It is also one of the most common business structures and it also has the potential to be costly. Not only is it costly financially but also because it's more susceptible to risk as there are no personal asset protections in place.

The main requirements to be a General Partnership besides being in one by default if you have 2 or more business owners, a business must have the required operating permits and documents which include a business license for the city they are operating in, but also a Fictitious Business Name (FBN) aka *Doing Business As (DBA)*, any industry required permits/licenses, sellers permit and etc. If you would like more information regarding what each of these items are, please see my other book: **Starting a Small Business – Step by Step Guide to Business Ownership.**

To avoid using your social security numbers and having it associated with the business, you can file for an Employee Identification Number (EIN). You do not have to have an employee or be in the middle of hiring one in order to file for an EIN.

This process is free and takes a few minutes. It is important to know which business entity you are currently in when filing for an EIN because it is one of the first questions on the form. Once you submit the form, you will be issued an EIN number which is a business identification number (similar to an individual's Social Security Number).

In this business structure, the owners have to share control according to the ownership percentages agreed upon whether it is 50/50, 60/40 or even 80/20. One good side about having a business partner is that there will be less personal investment as a piece of it will be shared with the other partner(s).

The downside is the decisions have to be decided between the partners and there will be times where there will be disagreements and yet somehow decisions need to still happen. Without a legally binding partnership agreement in place, a lot of problems do occur quickly before, after and during start-up.

A partnership agreement is a legally binding document that states the relationship characteristics of the business owners of a small business. It can include a lot of things such as percentage ownership, responsibilities and rights of each business partner, situational decisions such as what they will do if one partner wants out of the company, what they will do if one partner does not put in the same effort as everyone else, etc. Tough questions need to be asked and discussed between the partners before each person gets too excited about what having an incorrectly will be like before it starts.

The other drawback is that the owners have virtually no protection (other than business insurance – if it has enough coverage) that you are susceptible to losing any assets if you are involved in a lawsuit. What makes a general partnership worse is that as partners, they are one in the same. Partners can make decisions for the business without the other partner's agreement. Partners are considered one and the same person. Without adequate protection, it can be scary especially when your business partner can make decisions on your behalf.

As discussed earlier, a written partnership is recommended but not required. Each partner is an authorized agent of the business with equal responsibility and authority.

Each partner also reports share of the profits or losses in their income tax including the Schedule C.

Chapter 6

Limited Liability Partnership (LLP)

This is the unique entity out of the entire list as it takes dual characteristics, that of a Sole Proprietorship/Partnership but also that of a Corporation.

For this to be characterized as a Limited Liability Partnership (LLP), there needs to be at least one general partner and one limited partner. The general partner is responsible for managing the business and has unlimited liability.

The limited partner provides capital to start up or grow the business but their liability and operational responsibility is limited. With this entity, a partnership is also highly recommended but not essentially required.

Each partner will have to report their share of the profits or losses in their individual, personal income taxes. This business will have to register with the state and will be subject to a <u>minimum </u>of $800 state tax.

Chapter 7

Corporation – Sub Chapter C

A Corporation is the designation for the business entities/legal forms of business that enable the business owner to separate the personal assets form the business assets. As I've said before, there are some loop holes to this protection and exceptions but we will get to that later. For now, let's talk about some of the characteristics and the obligations of a Sub Chapter C Corporation.

A Sub Chapter C Corporation is required to file an "Articles of Incorporation" document with the Secretary of State. The forms can easily be found on the Secretary of State website for your individual state.

The Shareholders (Owners) of the C Corp have the right to vote and receive dividends.

With this business entity as we spoke of throughout the course of this book, Corporations provide limited liability to the owners of the business.

Limited liability is a term used for when the owners have very limited liability in case there is lawsuits against the business and the business owner in most cases will not be responsible for any business repercussions.

There is a double taxation element to the C Corp for both Federal and State Tax plus the $800 per year minimum tax.

Keep in mind when I refer to the $800 minimum tax that is a policy enforced by the State of California. Each STATE and CITY has its own tax requirements. Please keep this in mind.

A C Corp must create by laws (i.e. how the Corporation will operate) that covers items such as stockholder meetings, director meetings, number of officers and their responsibilities.

There needs to be a separate bank account and records required and the owners have ultimate control of the corporation, but must elect directors who in turn elect officers for the company. The directors make the major decisions, while the officers make the day-to-day decisions

Chapter 8

Corporation – Sub Chapter S

A Corporation is the designation for the business entities/legal forms of business that enable the business owner to separate the personal assets form the business assets. As I've said before, there are some loop holes to this protection and exceptions but we will get to that later. For now, let's talk about some of the characteristics and the obligations of a Sub Chapter S Corporation.

A Sub Chapter S Corporation is required to file an "Articles of Incorporation" document with the Secretary of State. The forms can easily be found on the Secretary of State website for your individual state.

The Shareholders (Owners) of the S Corp have the right to vote and receive dividends.

With this business entity as we spoke of throughout the course of this book, Corporations provide limited liability to the owners of the business. Limited liability is a term used for when the owners have very limited liability in case there is lawsuits against the business and the business owner in most cases will not be responsible for any business repercussions.

There is an $800 minimum state tax (CALIFORNIA ONLY) or a 1.5%, there is no Federal Tax.

Keep in mind when I refer to the $800 minimum tax that is a policy enforced by the State of California. Each STATE and CITY has its own tax requirements. Please keep this in mind.

Income of the company passes through the shareholders and there can only be a maximum of 100 shareholders. Another characteristic of the Sub Chapter S is that there should be no more than 25% income being passive and there also needs to be a separate bank account and records.

How a Corporation is Governed

- Stockholders elect Board of Directors.
- The Board of Directors select and supervise the Officers.

- The Officers run the day-to-day operations of the business.

- In smaller corporations, stockholders, directors and officers are often the same people.

- California requires at least two corporate officers (this varies by state).

Chapter 9

Limited Liability Company (LLC)

A Corporation is the designation for the business entities/legal forms of business that enable the business owner to separate the personal assets form the business assets. As I've said before, there are some loop holes to this protection and exceptions but we will get to that later. For now, let's talk about some of the characteristics and the obligations of a Sub Chapter S Corporation.

A Limited Liability Company (LLC) is required to file an "Articles of Incorporation" document with the Secretary of State. The forms can easily be found on the Secretary of State website for your individual state.

An LLC is also not required to hold annual meetings or file minutes like a Sub Chapter S or C Corporation. Members of the LLC are also not liable for obligations of the LLC (unless personally guaranteed).

An LLC also can elect to be taxed as a Sole Proprietorship, a Partnership or even a Corporation.

There is a minimum of $800 tax but keep in mind when I refer to the $800 minimum tax that is a policy enforced by the State of California. Each STATE and CITY has its own tax requirements. Please keep this in mind.

Chapter 10

Fictitious Business Name (FBN) / Doing Business As (DBA)

A Fictitious Business Name (FBN) statement also known as the *Doing Business As (DBA)* is required if you plan to operate your business under a name that differs from your company's legal name.

With a DBA you can legally open a bank account and also be able to conduct transactions using a trade name.

Other Forms of Business

- **Professional Service Corporations (PSC)** - Is an entity that must be organized for the sole purpose of providing a professional service for which each shareholder is licensed

- **Non Profit Corporation** – Is an entity that is formed for civic, educational, charitable, and religious purposes.

- This entity is not owned by the founders

- But it is governed by the board for the benefit of a particular community

Chapter 11

Checklist for Evaluating Legal Forms for Organization

Before deciding which entity you want to get into and evaluating legal forms, ask our self these questions:

- Under what legal form of organization is the company now operating?

- What are the major risks to which the company is subjected?

- Does the legal form give the proper protection against these risks?

- Is unlimited liability a serious potential problem?

- Does the company supplement its legal form of protection with public liability insurance?

- Has the present form limited financial needs in any way?

- What is the relative incidence of the company's major risks?

- Are there any tax advantages available by changing the legal form of organization?

- Have you considered the management advantages of alternative legal forms?

- Are you aware of the features of a Sub Chapter S corporation? Would they be beneficial?

- Is the company using all of the advantages of the present legal form of organization?